The Architecture of the
Washington Convention Center
Washington, D.C.

Civic Architecture in Support of
Urban Aspirations

The Architecture of the
Washington Convention Center
Washington, D.C.

Civic Architecture in Support of
Urban Aspirations

Planning, Architecture, and
Interiors by TVS

Essay by Deborah K. Dietsch
Foreword by Thomas W. Ventulett, III, FAIA

Edizioni Press

First published in the United States of America by Edizioni Press, Inc.
469 West 21st Street New York, New York 10011
www.edizionipress.com

ISBN: 1-931536-23-6

Library of Congress Catalogue Card Number: 2004117282

Printed in China

Design: Andrew Sloat
Editor: Sarah Palmer
Editorial Assistant: Nancy Sul

The Architecture of the
Washington Convention Center
Washington, D.C.

Civic Architecture in Support of
Urban Aspirations

Washington Preamble

By Thomas W. Ventulett, III, FAIA

At TVS we constantly remind ourselves to ask: What is the cause of a great work of architecture? We have found it to be, in fact, a constellation of causes—rather than a single cause—which gives rise to every great civic architectural work. These causes come both from within TVS and the other architectural firms charged with a building's commission, as well as from a civic consensus. Despite the oft-referenced cultural myth of the architect as a lone, embattled artist tilting a lance against the windmills of mediocrity, the complex discipline of civic architecture unites various minds and hands. During the design of any successful project, we find that a flash-point is reached where various aspirations congeal into a single, compelling vision that inspires human energy and financial capital on a Herculean scale.

Like most modern architecture firms, there exists a genealogy of form and concept in the body of our work, accompanied by a cross-pollination of projects contemporary to each other at any given period in the office. Thus, the ideas explored in one project may well be refined in subsequent projects, and drafting board camaraderie can give rise to shared explorations and resolutions on concurrent endeavors. These relationships, horizontal and vertical, require the incubator of a stable, continuous atelier or studio environment. One of the key ingredients to the continued success of TVS in its award-winning explorations and evolutions of multiple building types is the atelier-style structure of the firm. TVS today is an organization of 250 employees in three cities, organized into 20-odd ateliers under studio principals.

The convention center studio was cobbled together from a small staff of newly minted innocents in 1974 to serve the demands of one of the firm's first large commissions, what is now Phase One of the four-phase Georgia World Congress Center in Atlanta. Although the project and staff genealogy of that studio has many branches today, its core team played midwife to the evolutions of convention center program and design—from introverted box to extroverted participant in urban rejuvenation—for the ensuing 30 years. Looking back, the Georgia World Congress Center's Phases One (1974) through Four (2001) serve as a singular testimony to the evolutionary impact of TVS on the convention center building type.

However, it is in the new Washington Convention Center where 30 years of lessons learned and ambitions skillfully and beautifully tested serve the most challenging commission faced by the firm to date. From our work in Atlanta, TVS first developed and defined the functional diagram fundamental to the efficiency and marketability of a contemporary convention center, a diagram that is now standard of the industry. From our work on such convention center projects as Miami Beach (1988), Mobile (1993), and Charlotte (1995), the firm learned the artistic and political benefits of collaboration with local architects, a stance successfully brought forward in Washington, where TVS collaborated with both Devrouax & Purnell Architects and Mariani Architects Engineers.

Three key experiences gained in designing the award-winning Pennsylvania Convention Center in Philadelphia (1997) informed TVS's design process in Washington. First, the Philadelphia center called for the deft placement of a large footprint facility into the crossroads of an historically sensitive city center. TVS learned that building a public structure required, first and foremost, building a consensus, as the firm did through interactions with the Arts Commission, the AIA Urban Design Committee, and various city planning and advocacy groups. This lesson of consensus-building would serve the convention center studios well in their work with the National Capital Planning Commission (NCPC) and Commission of Fine Arts in Washington.

Second, in its conversion of the historic Reading Terminal train shed into a first class ballroom as an adjunct program to the Philadelphia center, TVS pursued the market enhancement of a dedicated formal ballroom as a memorable civic space—a lesson again brought forward in the elegant 56,000-square-foot ballroom in Washington.

And third, in an attempt to integrate the Philadelphia center into a concomitant development of neighboring upscale hotels, the TVS team elevated the palette of interior design aspirations and materials to the level of the anticipated hospitality market. The downtown location and design sophistication of this strategy have greatly aided in the rejuvenation of Philadelphia, and early evidence indicates a similar positive impact in Washington. From efforts at McCormick Place in Chicago (1999) the studio's—as well as the building type's—genetic code was altered in its evolutionary design response to issues of cohesive place-making and wayfinding on a mammoth scale. These lessons, important to enhancing visitor comfort during a day-long or multiple day stay at the facility, would serve the team well in the more than two million-square-foot challenge of the Washington Convention Center. Also, in Chicago as well as Philadelphia, a market program divided by the confines of urban sites equaled multi-level facilities with heavily loaded long-span structures placing exhibit space over meeting rooms. These lessons would in turn be dexterously applied to the six-block Mount Vernon Square site in central Washington.

All told, in its dedication to a single building type—which has resulted in the masterplanning and design of over 50 convention centers worldwide—TVS has transformed a city-snubbing, soulless box into a modern convention center that rewards and elevates the visitor, engenders surrounding development, and expresses the social mission of the building type—a place of commerce for human imagination.

Another myth in the realization of a great work of architecture is the myth of trajectory: that a building lands directly down-field from its original concept. Simply put, it is the myth of the napkin doodle. In reality, public projects spring from a civic launch pad and the trajectory is not a graceful arc but a jagged line subject to the winds and quirky gravities of the public agenda. In studying the evolution of a large-scale civic building—in sifting through the volume of the public record: meeting minutes of commissions, the proceedings of city councils, newspaper editorials, and purchasing contracts—one would determine that the most significant and influential decisions on a project are made by the commissions and agencies which act out of the common ground of civic altruism. Indeed, some of the most important decisions, such as conjecturing the very idea and scope of the project and establishing a site that is beneficial both to the building as well as the community at large, typically predate the purchasing contract for architectural services. And, once the design manifestation of the public agenda is underway by the architect, that work continues to be pushed about by various civic agendas like tugboats struggling to push an ocean liner to competing ports.

In Washington, several sites were considered by the public authorities prior to launching design work north of Mount Vernon Square in 1996. TVS, along with Devrouax & Purnell Architects, was engaged by the Convention Center Authority in 1985 for a study to determine the feasibility of expanding the existing center across New York Avenue, a site the team deemed an unsuitable match to the market program prepared by Gladstone Associates. In 1990, Mariani Architects Engineers collaborated with TVS on a study of the area north of Mount Vernon Square at the request of then-mayor Marion Barry. Additionally, a site behind Union Station was the subject of feasibility analysis by HNTB and others, and was under active consideration until the final civic consensus to proceed with the Mount Vernon Square site was reached in 1996.

In the "constellation of causes" behind a great building is an illuminated and focused civic leadership guiding the project to a safe and worthy port. In Washington, that constellation is made of many stars, but in particular two are the brightest: Harvey Gantt and the late J. Carter Brown. Mr. Gantt was the presidentially appointed chair of the National Capital Planning Commission. In his role as steward of the L'Enfant Plan, Mr. Gantt, an architect himself, knew that the challenges arising out of a respect for the L'Enfant grid and District of Columbia height restrictions would result in a richer, more inspired work of architecture. But, if there is one guiding star in the civic constellation, it was the encouraging and supportive Carter Brown. As a patron of outstanding civic architecture in America, Carter Brown used his position as chair of the Commission of Fine Arts to ensure that the civic expectations of the project were of the highest standards, and that the design team was inspired to abide by them.

Ultimately, in answering the question, "What is the cause of a great work of architecture?" the record of the Washington Convention Center would reveal that the dedication, skills, and imagination of the design team—Thompson, Ventulett, Stainback & Associates, Devrouax & Purnell Architects, and Mariani Architects Engineers—were aligned with the civic vision of the leaders of the District of Columbia, the Commission of Fine Arts, and the National Capital Planning Commission. It is in that celestial alignment, that constellation of causes, that human aspirations soar. ∎

An Exercise in Urban Infrastructure

By Deborah K. Dietsch

Unique among American cities, Washington, DC, reconfigures the grand plans of baroque Europe to the democratic purpose of our nation. Its framework of radiating avenues and orthogonal streets, designed in 1791 by Pierre Charles L'Enfant, connects centers of power—the White House and U.S. Capitol—to monuments, government buildings, commercial districts, and residential neighborhoods. Respect for L'Enfant's vision has guided the planning and design of downtown Washington for centuries, encouraging architects to defer to the urban context rather than to defy it.

For Atlanta architect Thompson, Ventulett, Stainback & Associates, the challenges of fitting the new Washington Convention Center into the capital's tradition-bound environment were enormous. By their very nature, convention centers are difficult to blend into any urban setting. Vast meeting halls demanding loading and staging requirements, the footprints of these huge buildings can overtake numerous city blocks and dwarf their surroundings. On the face of it, the Washington Convention Center seemed like no exception. Independent market studies for this giant building called for 2.3 million square feet of exhibition halls, conference rooms, and meeting spaces, and miles of corridors, making the building the largest in the city. Exhibit halls had to be tall and wide enough for huge displays and crowds, and positioned to stage both simultaneous and independent events with easy access for people and vehicles.

Compounding the difficulty of disguising the convention center's inherent size was its six-block site, which left no room to sprawl. The downtown parcels selected for the building, located in the District's Shaw neighborhood, are hemmed-in by historic rowhouses and other low-scale buildings. Moreover, the site lies in close proximity to the commercial and monumental cores of the city. Meeting the functional requirements necessary for such a huge building while weaving the architecture into this urban fabric posed an inherent contradiction.

"A lot of community people thought this convention center would overwhelm the neighborhood," says TVS Founding Principal Thomas Ventulett. "We not only had to think about the building but the total environment around it."

That meant mediating between the scale of the commercial and the residential blocks surrounding the site as well as establishing a grand, yet inviting presence related to Washington's family of monuments. Befitting its prominent location in the capital, the convention center was also expected to express national pride as the "people's living room." Both city and federal officials hoped it would be a welcoming, open, and accessible building representative of sophisticated urban design and democratic principles.

"Our building was expected to speak of the confidence of a law-abiding, democratic, and respectful civilization," says Ventulett. "Our design aspires to what is best in our society."

A tall order, indeed. TVS ably fulfilled its mission by applying its well-honed skills in convention center planning and design. Collaborating with the Washington firms of Mariani Architects Engineers and Devrouax & Purnell Architects, the firm used structural ingenuity and urban sensitivity to tap into the civic and social potential of the building type. "A convention center doesn't sound very inspiring to most people," points out Ventulett. "But as an efficient place for trade and commerce, it can create vitality within a city. It can be an exciting environment where people come together and interact. This is architecture that touches people's lives."

Reflecting its purpose as a social hub, the convention center achieves a human scale both inside and out that belies its jumbo size. Reducing the apparent building mass was accomplished by sinking the structure into the ground and preserving surrounding streets so they extend through the site. This approach was based on an overriding respect for Washington's historic city plan. "L'Enfant's plan guided our thinking," explains TVS Senior Principal C. Andrew McLean. "We tried to preserve the underlying urban grid by dividing the convention center into separate buildings that are one at the same time."

Maintaining the city's strict height restrictions also guided the sunken building design. Enacted by city commissioners in 1899 and amended by Congress in 1910, this height limitation requires structures to rise no higher than 110 feet along diagonal streets, and no more than 130 feet within the building mass. New structures within the heart of the city are also heavily scrutinized by federal agencies such as the Commission of Fine Arts and National Capital Planning Commission, as well as by municipal departments, preservation organizations, and citizen groups. Consensus-building among these groups, crucial to the approval of the project, helped to advance TVS's design, which required costly and difficult structural measures to succeed. Instead of becoming a big, bland box, the Washington Convention Center presents an inviting, variegated profile that's both monumental and neighborly, contemporary and respectful of tradition.

Respecting the Urban Fabric

Striking that balance was achieved through a lengthy process of planning, engineering, and fast-track construction that began in 1994 after the city decided to locate its new convention center on six vacant blocks owned by the District of Columbia. The site stretches north from the civic space of Mount Vernon Square to the low-rise structures along N Street. The square, quintessentially L'Enfant in configuration, is prominently located at the intersection of two diagonal boulevards connecting significant landmarks within the city: Massachusetts Avenue, which extends eastward to Union Station, and New York Avenue, which stretches westward to the White House. Situated at the center of its open space is the Carnegie Library, a 1902 Beaux-Arts landmark that served as the city's central library until 1972 and is now home to the City Museum of Washington, DC.

Moving northward from Mount Vernon Square, the orthogonal city grid is extended by three east-west streets established in the L'Enfant plan—L, M, and N Streets—that pass through the site. Bordering the convention center to the east is Washington's first commercial street, 7th Street, NW, and to the west is 9th Street, NW, which has replaced 7th Street as a major artery into the city.

Preserving the integrity of the street plan and the neighborhood scale was important to the architects and the community, especially given the failure of Washington's first convention center to mesh with its setting. That monolithic building, now demolished, was located one block southwest of the new convention center, and consumed portions of 10th and I Streets, obliterating the vistas carefully laid out by L'Enfant in his plan. Moreover, its featureless concrete façades acted as barriers to the surrounding commercial area.

Though this 800,000-square-foot convention center was the country's third largest when it opened in 1983, the bulky building quickly became obsolete. Cramped exhibit halls, shortage of meeting rooms, and lack of room to expand convinced city officials to build anew in a different location and avoid repeating the mute, anti-urban architecture of the outdated facility. "Our goal was to increase the size, flexibility, and utility [of the building], and to capture the pent-up demand for Washington, DC, as a convention destination," explains Bill Hanbury, President and CEO of the Washington, DC Convention and Tourism Corporation. Another of the city's aims was to create a new convention center with a high degree of transparency, not only to establish a more inviting image but to highlight the activity inside so the public would be aware of their tax dollars at work.

To build the new $834 million complex, the DC government taxed area hotels and restaurants to secure $507 million worth of bonds. Financing also came from federal and local grants, contracts with vendors, and interest earnings. Careful consideration was also paid to the scheduling of events in the building so as to maximize its use. Most convention centers house exhibit halls on one floor, but Washington didn't have the space for such a continuous venue on the site for its new center. Instead of building one huge hall for large events, the building is organized with halls on two levels. This organization makes it easy to host several simultaneous events. This way, both events may be in session or activities can be staggered, and in different modes of move-in, in-session, or move-out. This split-hall approach better reflected the very reason behind building the new convention center—to put "heads in beds" and bring more tourist dollars to the city. By avoiding the peaks associated with one large show, hotels would have a more consistent level of occupancy over a longer period of time.

After being selected as the lead architect of the new convention center in 1996, TVS worked with the National Capital Planning Commission and Commission of Fine Arts to establish an overall strategy for design and construction. "These regulatory agencies became our allies," says McLean. "They had the same aspirations as the design team. We were in sync about the retention of the streets, the quality of materials, and the level of architecture for the building. Once our design was approved by these agencies, there was no going back."

TVS approached the six-block site chosen for the new Washington Convention Center with the same contextual dexterity as applied to many of its previous architectural designs. Over the past three decades, the firm has completed 50 convention and conference centers in cities

all over the country. Designing the award-winning Pennsylvania Convention Center in downtown Philadelphia proved especially relevant in shaping Washington's huge urban facility. This 1.3 million-square-foot structure, opened in 1997, incorporates a landmark train shed and responds to its historic surroundings with rhythmic bays constructed of brick and stone. Façades are designed with bow windows, moldings, and distinctive entrances to respect the architectural character of the train shed and street frontage adjacent to the building.

TVS's experience in adding three million square feet to Chicago's McCormick Place Convention Center, completed in 1996, also proved beneficial. Similar in size to Washington's new center, the South Hall expansion required bold urban design maneuvers, including the creation of a five-acre public square, to connect the complex to Chicago's cultural institutions and surrounding neighborhoods. "Having worked on Chicago," notes TVS Principal R. Scott Sickeler, "our team was better prepared for the technical and urban challenges of Washington."

In Washington, TVS sought to integrate the massive convention center into the urban fabric by preserving as much of the city grid as possible. Rather than subsume L and M Streets into the building, the architects extended these east-west routes right through the convention center. This division helped reduce the building mass by separating the long structure into three volumes, which are connected by enclosed pedestrian walkways over the streets at the upper stories. In addition to respecting the L'Enfant Plan, maintaining the cross streets allows for unimpeded traffic flow, pedestrian connections through the neighborhood, and additional access points for bus and taxi drop-offs.

Another smart planning decision was to lessen the impact of the immense complex by burying 40 percent of the building below grade. Moving two-thirds of the exhibit space down instead of up lessened the height and the mass of the structure while providing a 500,000-square-foot subterranean hall serviced by underground loading docks and sunken concourses. It also ensured that the building would not present huge, blank walls and rows of exit doors to the street, but could incorporate windows to flood concourses and public areas with sunshine—a benefit typically absent in many convention centers.

Shaping the Super-sized Structure

Putting the biggest room at the lowest level required digging a gigantic hole that extended, on average, 50 feet into the earth and 25 feet into the water table. The excavation, billed as the largest for a new building in the Western Hemisphere, necessitated removing two million tons of dirt from the site while bringing in structural steel, concrete, and other materials to shore up surrounding streets and buildings. On site every day was an army of 1,100 hard-hat workers, supervised by the construction management firm Clark/Smoot, to ensure building proceeded apace. "Planning, designing, and constructing the new Washington Convention Center has been an extraordinary challenge involving hundreds of contractors and consultants, but the results have been worth it," says Allen Y. Lew, Managing Director of Development for the Washington Convention Center Authority. "From the early conceptual design phase to the phenomenal effort during the construction phase, our architects worked in concert with the construction management and subcontractor teams to achieve the completion schedule on time. We were able to keep within our budget and close out the trades with no claims, liens, or lawsuits."

Around the perimeter, a continuous slurry wall that extended as deep as 75 feet in some areas was poured and laterally braced by 115-foot-long steel compression struts to hold back the forces of adjacent earth and water. Designed by Mueser Rutledge Consulting Engineers, this 3.5-foot-thick wall, which acts as an inverted bathtub, extends under 9th Street to 25 feet shy of the foundations of historic rowhouses and other properties on the western side of the street. It also abuts an adjacent subway station and tunnels running the full length of the 7th Street edge and a preserved apartment block on the building's eastern side. In addition to the slurry wall, the foundation consists of spread footings, support columns, and interior shear walls.

Framed in a 38,000-ton steel super-structure, the building is divided into 90-foot by 90-foot bays supported by built-up columns and deep trusses. "Every single square foot of the lowest level is a long span, and, thereby, first class exhibition space," explains Sickeler. "The challenge was putting another long-span space over that to create the upper exhibit hall. If you don't figure out the structure from the onset, structural demands will come back to overwhelm the interior spaces." Stacking the long-span spaces required enormous struts and 14-foot-deep trusses, resulting in a floor-to-floor dimension as large as 34 feet. This super-size structure meant expansion joints, some nearly a foot wide, had to be placed between the different building blocks to allow

for structural deflection and movement. Precast concrete and limestone veneered façades necessitated a separate tubular steel structure and 55-foot-high exposed trusses to brace the entrance façade's glass curtainwall.

Construction proceeded from the north and south ends into the middle of the building, requiring so much steel—enough for seven Eiffel Towers—that structural elements were fabricated in seven places, including China, Russia, and South Korea. With the shipping of the steelwork came some unfortunate mishaps. In 2000, a shipment of roof trusses from Korea was jettisoned at sea when the vessel carrying the load lost power during a storm. The trusses were subsequently remanufactured in the United States. A year later, 14 more trusses were remade after high winds and inadequate temporary bracing caused part of the roof structure to topple. Despite these setbacks, construction proceeded on schedule to meet the deadline set for the building's opening in March 2003.

Establishing a Civic Presence

TVS took advantage of the sloping site, which rises to the north, to stack ballroom, meeting spaces, and support areas vertically, and reduce walking and "exhibit fatigue." The slope also allowed the building to be appropriately shaped into a higher, monumental portion along Mount Vernon Square and gradually descend in height to its lowest profile along N Street, which matches the scale of rowhouses and smaller structures to the north. Roof heights range from 40 feet at the north end to 110 feet at the south, with a height of 135 feet at the center of the site where higher sections are shaped into curved vaults to recede from view.

Neighborliness is not often associated with convention centers, but TVS skillfully broke down the horizontal mass of its building with varied, street-friendly façades that acknowledge the historic, late 19th-century architecture around the site. Along 7th and 9th Streets, rounded bays, changing window patterns, canopies, and overhanging cornices give the impression that the huge center is composed of separate but related buildings. "The intention was to reinforce the vertical aspects of the façades to recall the narrow widths of rowhouses," points out Sickeler. Crisply outlined with repeated geometric details, the glass and light-colored masonry façades achieve a cohesive expression that is clearly contemporary and does not mimic its older neighbors.

Exterior elements and materials are finely tuned to the particulars of context. As the building extends northward into the residential Shaw neighborhood, for example, Norman brick walls become more prevalent to harmonize with adjacent masonry buildings. Activity within the building is also taken into account. On the north façade along N Street, upper-level truck docks are screened by translucent glass panels. Along the sidewalk, storefronts are built in to anticipate street-level retail and restaurants. The convention center jogs inward at its northeast corner on 7th Street to accommodate the McCollough Terrace Apartments, a subsidized housing block that was left intact. The façade abutting the rear yard and alley of the apartment building incorporates cable trellises and planters to form a garden wall that will turn green with life.

Fronting Mount Vernon Square, the convention center's exterior takes a more formal turn to acknowledge the monuments of the federal city. This inward-curving, civic frontispiece is symmetrically arranged and framed by limestone piers at the corners, a clear nod to the classical architecture of the historic Carnegie Library within the square. The front façade is the only place in the convention center where symmetry rules—the rest of the exterior is asymmetrically composed—and it's a surprisingly bold stroke given the building's modernist slant.

While taking cues from its historic neighbor, the Mount Vernon façade is made almost entirely of glass to establish a transparent, contemporary counterpoint to the classical solidity of the marble library. This giant window provides inviting glimpses into the lobby during the day, while becoming a beacon of light at night. On the upper levels, glassy bays jutting past the stone corner piers extend the play of transparency and reflectivity beyond the building envelope. These cantilevered corners reinforce the vistas of L'Enfant's plan (and provide views of the Capitol and Washington Monument from the interior) by creating a memorable silhouette that can be seen from a distance along the diagonals of New York and Massachusetts Avenues.

And it's clear where the front door is. Accentuating the entrance are towering, tapered pylons made of granite and stacked glass, which shimmers green in the sunlight and is lit from within at night, while at the same time acting as a portal to its continuation within the building's interior. These piers flank the main promenade through the building along an axis once occupied by 8th Street to symbolically mark the civic termination of this important street. A chain connecting some of Washington's most iconic classical buildings, 8th Street runs from the National Archives northward to the former U.S. Patent Office (home to the National Portrait Gallery and National Museum of American Art), Carnegie Library, and now to the new convention center.

Directing Visitors through Design

Convention centers are often derided for their windowless rooms and mazelike corridors. TVS worked hard to counter this introspective stereotype with design moves that orient visitors and put them in touch with city views. Interiors are designed as a cityscape with "streets," "monuments," and vistas so that the building is understandable to all users—no matter what language they speak—without having to rely on signs. Glazing and clerestories are positioned to fill concourses and pre-function areas with daylight. Windows in public areas supply a sense of the outdoors from the inside, and, from the street, views of convention activity inside the building. Throughout, custom-designed fixtures and finishes create an atmosphere of fine hospitality rather than institutional economy. "We tried to create a comfort level for the visitor," says Sickeler. Elements on the outside are repeated inside, such as the large, curved bays, so you always know where you are. Throughout the building, features are designed so you remember them and won't get lost."

From the entrance, a spacious civic room welcomes visitors into the complex and sets the tone for the entire complex. Skylights and a glass entrance wall flood the 90-foot-tall space with daylight so that the lobby is clearly visible from the street and made to feel inviting and accessible. Soaring upward to frame the space is a 60-foot-tall curved wall of African makore wood that acts as a solid complement to the transparent entrance façade.

Standing in this grand room, a visitor immediately understands the building's disposition of spaces. Straight down the center of the lobby, a concourse leads to stairs and escalators rising to the main assembly hall. To the left, a staircase descends to the lower exhibit hall. Turning right, a large staircase invites visitors to ascend to the ballroom on the upper floor with a tapering sweep that celebrates the vertical organization of the building. Overhead, bridges connecting the floors above infuse the space with a sense of activity by revealing glimpses of conventioneers on their way to meetings.

The new center incorporates a unique stacked arrangement of exhibit halls and meeting spaces that permits several exhibits and shows to be hosted at the same time. Elevated above the 500,000-square-foot

lower exhibit space is a 200,000-square-foot hall, located in the northern two-thirds of the building. This space can be subdivided by movable partitions into two rooms for smaller shows and political assemblies. Separate loading and service areas for the subterranean and above-ground halls allow convenient and efficient truck access to each hall division. Meeting rooms are sandwiched on the floors between the exhibit halls, making them accessible to each hall, and are placed at street level to provide daylight, easy exiting, and animation at the street.

Connecting the convention halls and the meeting spaces are day-lit, spacious lobbies and concourses that lead visitors through the building and put them in touch with the city. The main route providing access to the subterranean exhibit hall and connecting it to the upper-level assembly hall, which allows for heavy traffic flow during a single event, is a wide concourse, sunken 20 feet below grade. This passageway parallels 9th Street and extends under L and M Streets, but doesn't feel like it's underground. Structural maneuvering allowed the architects to maximize its ceiling height and frame the space with tall windows so visitors are unaware they are walking below two streets. To reach this corridor from the assembly hall on the upper level, visitors descend from lobbies and escalators built within glassy "rotundas." These curved bays, individually expressed within the 9th Street façade, further link the interior with the outdoors by supplying daylight, views, and orientation points.

Atop the south wing fronting Mount Vernon Square is a 56,000-square-foot ballroom—one of the largest on the East Coast—that's designed with the luxurious feeling of a grand old hotel. The refinement of the large space, which can be subdivided into three smaller rooms, is unusual for a convention center but perfectly appropriate for this ballroom, where events like inaugural balls and political fundraisers are held. As if to underscore its national purpose, the pre-function area outside the ballroom offers views of the U.S. Capitol dome and the Washington Monument. Much of visual interest inside the ballroom is supplied by a vaulted ceiling covered in an intricate latticework of plaster-like glass-reinforced gypsum. In addition to providing architectural detail, the latticework serves to baffle sound and conceal speakers, lighting equipment, fire detectors, sprinklers, and rigging points. Makore wood paneling and colorfully patterned carpets within the space contribute to the elegant décor.

Throughout the huge complex, floors and ceilings are patterned with geometric motifs that repeat elements of the architecture and provide

distinctive visual cues for visitors. "From the exterior detailing down to the carpet, we created a consistent language that allowed for variety," notes architect and interior designer Liz Neiswander, Principal of TVS Interiors. "The idea was to make an environment that was memorable enough that you minimized the need for applied graphics or signage." In front of the main expo hall, for example, portions of the ceiling project into the concourse to mark the entrances to the huge space.

The convention center's cavernous spaces are further humanized by a diverse array of sculptures, paintings, photography, graphics, and multimedia works. By programming art into the architectural design, TVS ensured that a variety of contemporary expressions would be accommodated. "Typically, the only art that makes sense for a convention center is a huge, site-specific installation," points out Neiswander. "We modulated the architecture to allow more artists to participate and complete smaller pieces." Larger pieces are mounted in heavily trafficked concourse and entrance areas, while more intimate works are displayed in niches within concourses and vitrines adjacent to meeting rooms.

Assembling this $4 million public art collection, the largest in any convention center, was accomplished by the DC Commission on the Arts and Humanities, Chicago art consultant Joel Straus, and a team of local art experts and museum curators. The group selected both local and nationally recognized talents to create pieces for more than 80 locations in the building. About 20 artworks were specifically commissioned to match the scale of prominent circulation spaces.

Many of the larger, site-specific artworks deliver a strong, visual punch to double as way-finding devices. Greeting visitors at street level is a pair of imposing bronze columns by Washington sculptor Jim San-

born. Beckoning from the escalator to the second floor exhibit hall is a brightly striped mural by artist Sol LeWitt that wraps around a circular staircase. In front of the two-story windows on the lower concourse is a star-studded glass sculpture by local artist Larry Kirkland and floating nearby is Kendall Buster's biomorphic assembly of shade cloth and steel. Scattered within the Grand Lobby are Donald Lipski's abstractly shaped *Five Easy Pieces*. More than half of the collection comprises artworks by area artists, including vibrant pieces by neighborhood talents displayed along a corridor dubbed the Shaw Wall.

Expected to attract three million visitors annually, the new convention center is predicted to generate 17,000 jobs and $1.4 billion a year for the Washington area economy through tax revenues and visitor expenditures. A recent report issued by the Washington Convention Center Authority suggests that early economic impact projections may be conservative and that spending on hotel accommodations, dining, and entertainment will total approximately $328.4 million in 2003. "With the opening of the new convention center, the city and this community will experience significant economic growth," says Mayor Anthony A. Williams. "The new convention center has already had a major impact on this community by utilizing local resources to help construct one of the finest convention facilities in the world."

After nearly a decade of planning, design, and construction, Washington's new meeting place achieves what few thought this vast structure could do: It has become a civic monument and a good neighbor. TVS has fine-tuned its expertise in convention center design to create a building that respects context and promotes community. This well-groomed giant sets a precedent for other cities to follow. ∎

Exterior

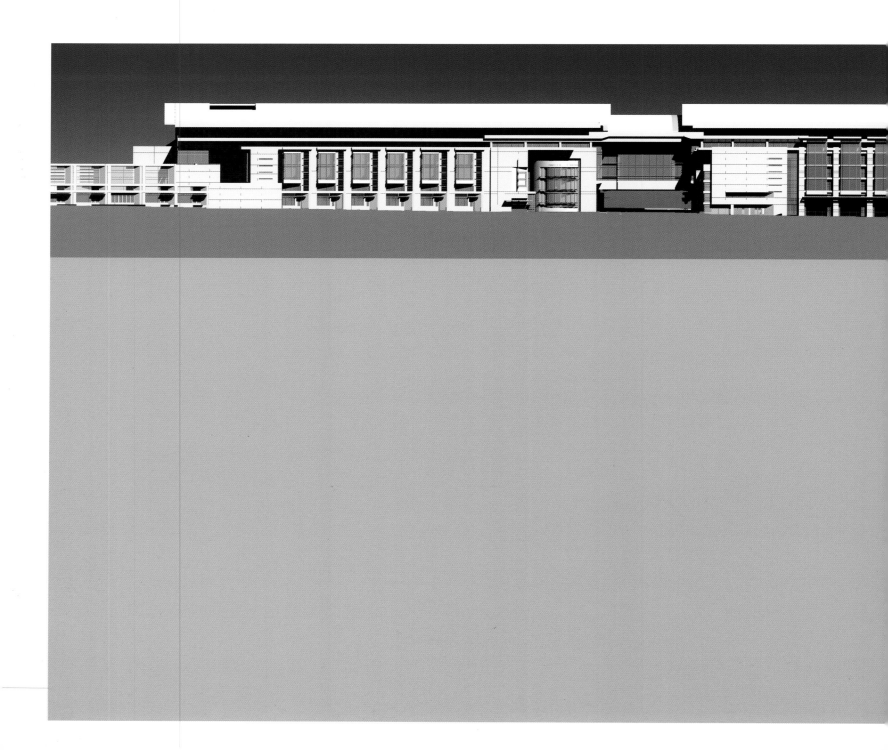

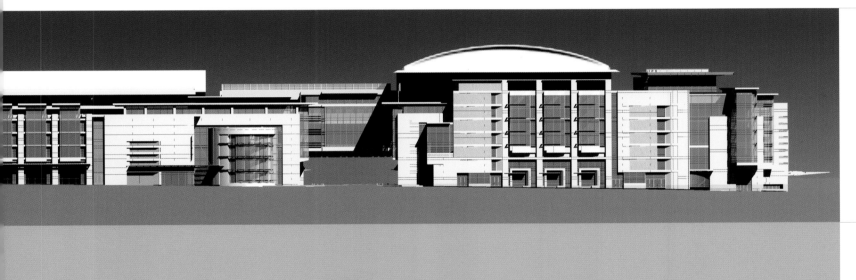

◀ *The principal façade on Mount Vernon Square*
reflects the symmetries of the L'Enfant Plan for the
District of Columbia and the classical architecture
of the neighboring Carnegie Library.

▼ *Limestone and stacked glass pylons honor the former 8th Street*
axis linking the National Archives and National Portrait Gallery
to the Navy Memorial on Pennsylvania Avenue.

*◄ The street grid of Pierre Charles L'Enfant's master
plan of 1791 is preserved by placing the main
exhibit hall below grade and envisioning sections
of the public concourses as transparent bridges.*

▲ *A gradual diminution of building height reflects the change northward along 9th Street from a civic to a neighborhood context.*

▼ *Views down the obliquely intersecting New York and Massachusetts Avenues can be enjoyed from the projecting ends of the Grand Lobby on Mount Vernon Square.*

◄ *A weave of Indiana limestone and brick allows the building to bridge between the monumental and residential.*

◄ *A new Metro station and public retail components along 7th Street mask the elevated truck docks serving the Upper Assembly Hall.*

◄ *The Upper Assembly Hall passes over M Street,*
which is preserved in respect to the L'Enfant Plan.

▲ *The limestone, granite, and glass of the Mount Vernon Square façade position the convention center as one in the District of Columbia's family of monuments.*

Level One

Grand Lobby

Registration

Meeting Rooms

Metro Station

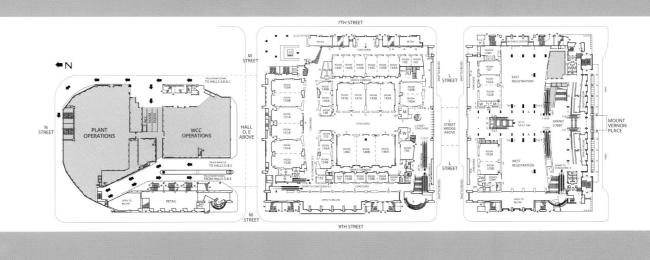

Level One

▲ *A concourse along the axis of 8th Street elevates the visitor from the Grand Lobby to the Upper Assembly Hall.*

▶ *Shafts of sunlight enliven the arcing wood wall of the Grand Lobby and the cascading stairs from the Grand Ballroom.*

◄ Although the lobby is one of the grandest public spaces in the nation's capital, intimate conversations are accommodated in lounges nestled within the monumental architecture along Mount Vernon Square.

45

► *With the largest public art collection in Washington, DC, the convention center boasts installations such as* Lingua *by Jim Sanborn, which serve as orienting waypoints along the public concourses.*

▼ *Meeting room interiors are of a stature and*
elegance befitting hospitality in the nation's capital.

Level One

▼ *Glass vitrines at meeting*
room entrances accommodate
changing art installations and
assist in visitor way-finding.

◄ *Significant art installations, such as Larry Kirkland's*
Capital Stars *glow in the natural light of the rotundas*
that mark the crossings of the public concourses.

9th Street Concourse

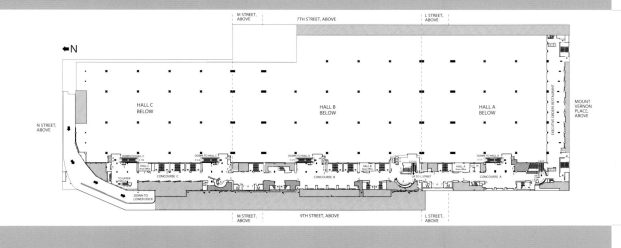

9th Street Concourse

▶ Five Easy Pieces *by Donald Lipski announces the start of the 9th Street Concourse from the Grand Lobby.*

▶ *Abundant daylight offers a
respite from the light sensitive
exhibit halls and meeting
rooms accessed off the grand
9th Street Concourse.*

Hall A

▲ *Intimate areas for impromptu
conversations occur along the
9th Street Concourse beneath
the crossing city streets of the
L'Enfant Plan.*

Lower Level   **Main Exhibit Hall**

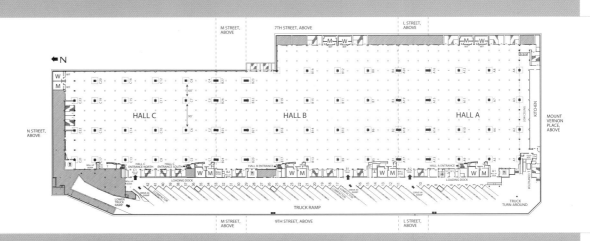

N

HALL C

HALL B

HALL A

M STREET, ABOVE

7TH STREET, ABOVE

L STREET, ABOVE

N STREET, ABOVE

MOUNT VERNON PLACE, ABOVE

HALL C ENTRANCE NORTH

HALL C ENTRANCE SOUTH

HALL B ENTRANCE

HALL A ENTRANCE

LOADING DOCK

LOADING DOCK

KITCHEN

TRUCK RAMP

TRUCK TURN-AROUND

LOWER TRUCK RAMP

M STREET, ABOVE

9TH STREET, ABOVE

L STREET, ABOVE

Lower Level

▲ *The descent from the 9th Street Concourse to the Lower Exhibit Hall is marked by five stair and escalator pods, each of which offers orientation to the visitor both from above and within the vast 500,000-square-foot hall.*

Level Two

Meeting Rooms

L Street Bridge

Exhibit Assembly Hall

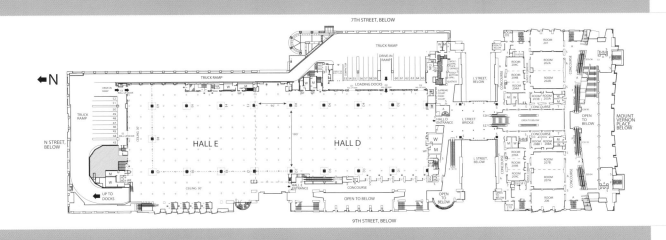

N

Level Two

▶ *Sol LeWitt's* Wall Drawing #1103 *vibrantly colors the visitor's experience of the circular stair tower connecting the levels between meeting rooms and the Upper Assembly Hall.*

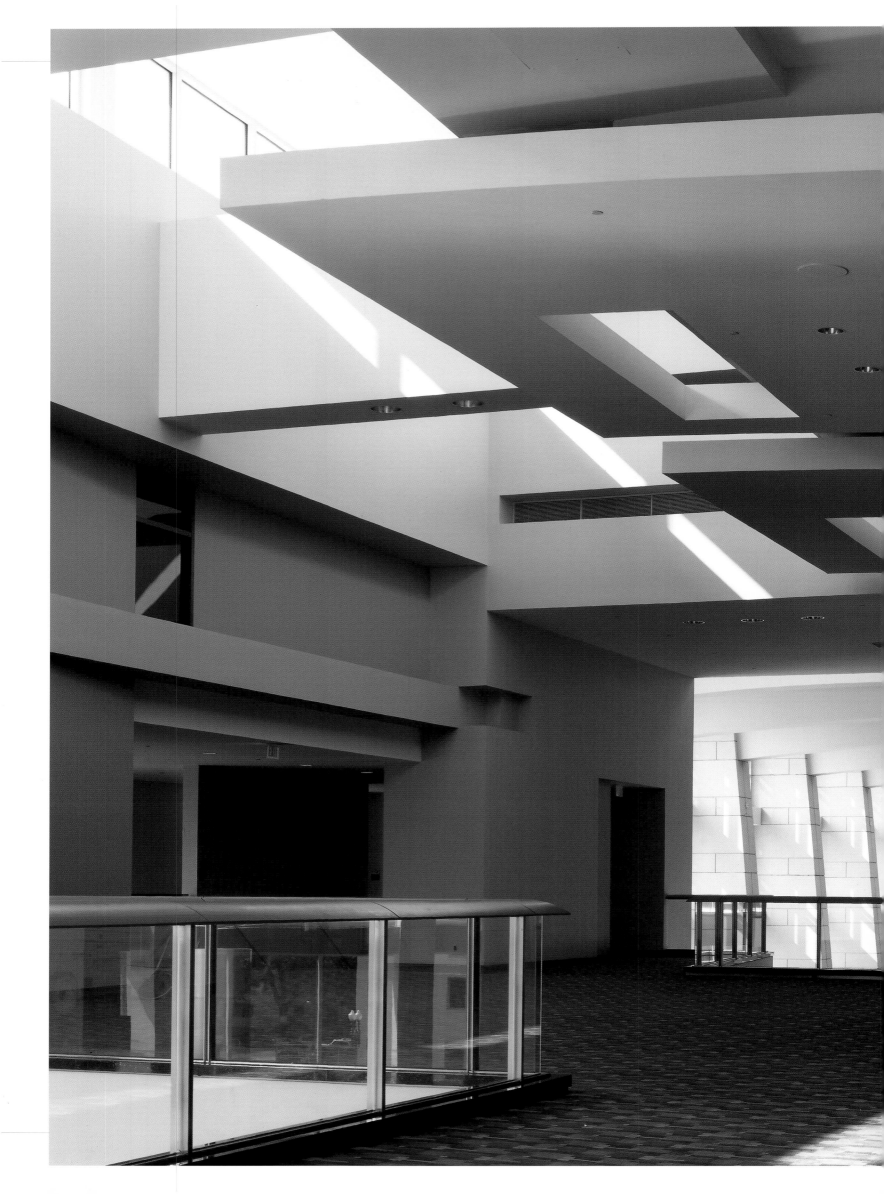

▲ *Natural light dramatically
activates the 80-foot-tall
monumental columns along
the 9th Street Concourse.*

▶▶ *(overleaf) The form, finishes, and technology of the Upper Assembly Hall accommodate exhibition, plenary, and banquet events.*

▶ *The detailed geometry of the exterior architecture is transposed into the patterns and materials of the interior palette.*

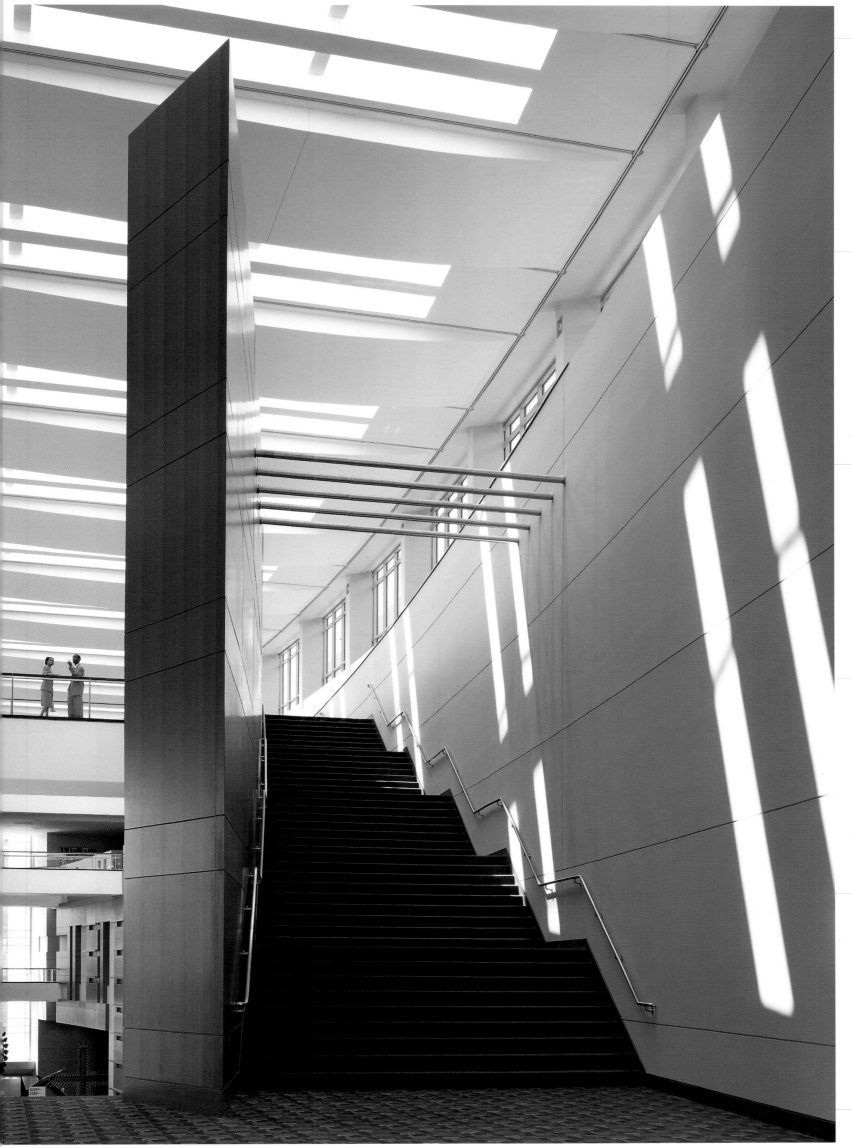

Level Three

Grand Ballroom

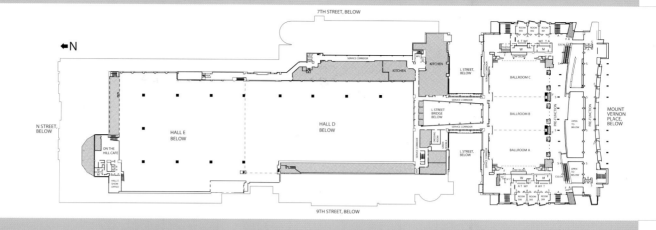

N

Level Three

◀ *The ascent to the ballroom is rewarded by the spatial drama of the Grand Lobby and memorable views to the monuments of the nation's capital.*

▶ Views from the concourses and lobbies offer the visitor a connection to the District of Columbia and its varied architecture.

Ballroom

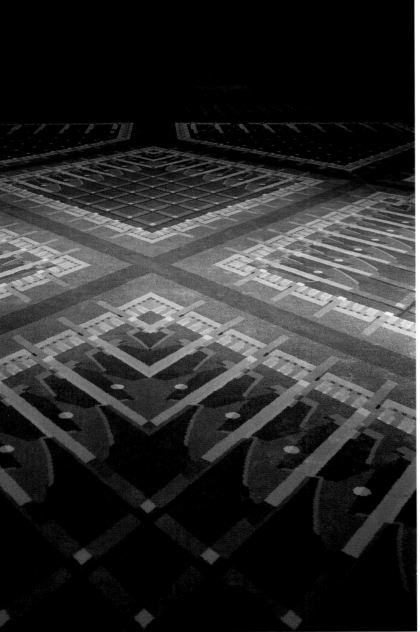

◄ *A language woven of form, material, pattern, and detail culminates in the Grand Ballroom, 60 feet above street level, befitting its role as the premier venue for gala events of State.*

Credits

Thompson, Ventulett, Stainback & Associates

Thomas W. Ventulett, FAIA, C. Andrew McLean, FAIA, Roger Neuenschwander, FAIA, R. Scott Sickeler, AIA, Liz Neiswander, AIA, Ken Stockdell, Jr., AIA, Mike Hagen, AIA, Kevin Gordon, AIA, Mike Azumi, Associate AIA, Peter Green, AIA, Scott Morris, AIA, Don Benz, AIA, CSI, Kyoko Iwasaka, Yon Jung, William Martin, AIA, Ingrida Martinkus, Foreman Rogers, NCIDQ, Binh Truong, Susan Reynolds, Sonny Crowe, Dots Colley, Eric Richey, Rainier Simoneaux, Leo Nourachi, John Fretwell, Laura Davis, Albert Chang, Alex Pfeiffer, Chris Jones, John Works, Anthony Guaraldo, Richard Ortiz, Chris Lepine. *Consultants*: Tim Hudgins, Bill Griffin, Richard Sachs, Phillip Andrews, Jason Bourgeois, Richard Adams, Gabriel Alvarado

Devrouax & Purnell

Paul S. Devrouax, FAIA, Marshall E. Purnell, FAIA, Anthony Brown, Marc Doswell, RA, Monier Barakat, Kelvin Harris, Sean Pichon, Umakant Gajjar, Wade McKinney, Richard Hines, Cynthia Hamlin, Sheronne Mason, Sigidi Mbonisi, Anne Brown, Wayne Cecil, Karen Ostromecki, Harash Vashishat

Mariani Architects Engineers

Theodore F. Mariani, FAIA/PE, Karim Najjar, RA, George Kousoulas, AIA, Richard Powers, RA, Mara Newsom, RIBA, Theodore M. Mariani, RA, Reginald H. Cude, AIA, Homayoun Kazempiour, Eric Peterson, Patrick Darnell, Shoukouh Amin-Khalilian, Suana Schoen, Mary R. Rankin, Matthias Teut, Tatiana Gloukhoff, Edward Defandorf, RA.

Client

Washington Convention Center Authority

Consultants

Structural
James Madison Cutts, Ross Bryan Associates, Daniels and Associates (Building Superstructure), Mueser Rutledge Consulting Engineers (Slurry Walls & Foundations), Jackson & Tull (Road Structure)

Mechanical, Electrical, and Security
John J. Christie & Associates; Henry Adams, Inc.

Civil
Jackson & Tull

Geotechnical
Schnabel Engineering Associates, Inc.

Environmental
Horne Engineering

Landscape
Lee & Liu Associates

Interior Design
TVS Interiors

Lighting
C.M. Kling & Associates

Food Service
Cini-Little International

Graphics
Jones-Worley Design, Inc.

Acoustics/Audio-visual
Acentech, Inc.

Cost
Leonard Smith Associates, Inc.

Code
Howe Engineers

Acknowledgments

Telecommunications / Data
Tilden Lobnitz Cooper, Inc.

Communications
Anderson, Inc.

Curtainwall
Advanced Structures, Inc.

Building Maintenance

Citadel Consulting, Inc.

Construction Manager

Clark/Smoot, Joint Venture

Project Manager

Convention Center Associates including
JBG, HNTB, and Turner Construction

Photography

Brian Gassel, TVS

TVS would like to express sincere appreciation to our associate architects, Mariani Architects Engineers and Devrouax & Purnell Architects, who partnered in the design of the largest public building in the nation's capital. The Washington Convention Center was perhaps the most ambitious and challenging architectural commission that any of the firms had undertaken. From the earliest exploratory meetings with neighborhood leaders and public authorities to the final ribbon-cutting ceremony in 2003, the design team collaborated to create a distinctive and complementary urban environment.

Concurrently, the civic leadership on this enormous project was steadfast. The challenge of designing and integrating a massive complex into the existing context of neighboring buildings required tireless consensus-building. The leadership within the Fine Arts Commission and the National Capital Planning Commission was pivotal in bringing citizen and preservation groups and federal and municipal agencies together to ensure that everyone could take pride in the new Washington emblem.

Anthony Iannacci and Sarah Palmer of Edizioni Press were patient and supportive in the making of this book. They offered creative means of portraying, through words and imagery, the intricacies of this large building.

Brian Gassel, TVS's own photographer, continues to produce wonderful photography of the firm's architectural and interior design projects. He was intricately involved in the decisions surrounding the design and imagery within this book. Kevin Gordon, one of TVS's most talented designers, pitched in and contributed to some of the writing and imagery of the book.

We express appreciation and thanks to the talented and dedicated staff, both past and present, who have contributed to the firm's reputation for design excellence.